BORROWING TIME

In memory of
Richard Kay

MICHAEL BURRELL

BORROWING TIME

AMBER LANE PRESS

All rights whatsoever in this play are strictly reserved
and application for performance, etc. must be made
before rehearsals begin to:

Margaret Ramsay Ltd.
14a Goodwin's Court
St. Martins Lane
London WC2N 4LL

No performance may be given unless a licence has been
obtained.

First published in 1990 by
Amber Lane Press Ltd
Cheorl House
Church Street
Charlbury, Oxon OX7 3PR

Telephone: 0608 810024

Typeset in Baskerville by
Oxonian Rewley Press Ltd., Oxford

Printed in Great Britain by
Bocardo Press Ltd., Didcot, Oxfordshire

Copyright © Michael Burrell, 1990
ISBN 0 906399 97 1

CHARACTERS

RICHARD FARNSWORTH
JUDITH FARNSWORTH: his wife
JOHN HOCKADAY: Judith's father
LILIAN HOCKADAY: John's sister

ACT ONE: *In Harness*

A house in suburban London in the late 1950's

JUDITH: ⎫
RICHARD: ⎬ both aged about 30

ACT TWO: *Letting Go*

Around 1980

Scene 1: John Hockaday's house
Scene 2: His room in a nursing home

JUDITH: early fifties
JOHN: late seventies

ACT THREE: *Sands*

A beach in East Anglia during the Great War

LILIAN: aged 17
JOHN: aged 15

NOTE: The play is written with the intention that all parts should be played by one actor and one actress.

Borrowing Time was first presented at Université Ain Chock, Casablanca, on 22nd February 1988, under the auspices of the British Council. It was directed by Philip Grout and the parts were played by Michael Burrell and Barbara Ferris.

The play was first presented in London at the Latchmere Theatre, Battersea on 25th April 1990, with the same cast and director.

FOREWORD

At first glance these might appear to be three one-act plays strung together under an umbrella title. In performance, for which like all plays *Borrowing Time* is written, the interdependence of the structure is clearer. Each scene changes the understanding of what has gone before. As in life themes and events, even what we call facts, come into focus and become different with hindsight.

The structure is deliberately spare, like Chinese wire pictures, never more than two characters present at a time; partly for artistic reasons but, as often with the arts, primarily for practical and economic ones. Like most family games it can be played by any number between two and six and this flexibility makes presentation and touring of the piece of interest to a range of groups.

I am sometimes asked about the time sequence. In each act there is some deliberate literary fun with the period of its setting. The fifties I remember providing a number of small scale earnest family dramas, something short of torrid. And the references in the first act are accurate: there was an Embassy cinema in North Harrow which disappeared like the excellent Harrow Coliseum theatre to become a supermarket; many railway bridges over suburban main roads around London were replaced in the way described, and such mundane events were sometimes used by playwrights of the period for small scale symbolism. Wall-to-wall carpeting, black-and-white televisions, along with washing machines which do not get a mention, were the first emblems of consumerism, sought after and prized by a generation determined to be treated better than its forbears.

Similarly the other acts reflect the topical concerns of their periods. The beginning of the twentieth century and the end of the nineteenth was the time when school stories were at the height of their popularity in Britain and this gives an appropriateness to young Lilian and John as prime movers. The schools they attend are fictitious, but unquestionably real, and the prizes John wins certainly existed, one of them named for just such a young inexperienced officer whose life like millions of others was tossed on the scrap heap in the First World War.

And the eighties have seen an increasingly ageing population in this particular country and the advent of hospices where death can be approached with some dignity and honesty. Though, given the period's political leadership, such comforts are only for the few who like John can afford them.

The language and the dialogue throughout reflect the usage of the time and I will leave it to literary students to detect what other writers may have formed an influence.

The reason for the non-chronological order of events is that it comes closest to life's realities. The play is concerned with relationships, death, perceptions of truth, loneliness, gender roles, many of the things which occupy, confuse and sometimes destroy us. As we go through life we come to a few decisions of our own and sadly put up a few shutters of our own, too. It is not unusual to think we know more about things as we become older; but as John finds in Act Two the world we inhabit changes and we may in truth know less. Always there is a new generation pushing up with its own dogmatism, its own ideals and doubts and certainties. The outsider, like the audience, might know how they are going to end up, but the young crash in like the waves on the beach, assertive, renewing, and refreshing even in their clichés.

Michael Burrell
Norfolk
June 1989

ACT ONE

In Harness

JUDITH *and* RICHARD*'s living room. There is a door off to the hallway and stairs. Children's things and the remains of tea are to be seen.*

JUDITH *comes in and starts clearing away, tidying up in the course of the ensuing.*

JUDITH: [*surveying the room*] A woman's place is in a home. Look at it. Well, look at me.

[*She clears items onto a tray.*]

'The daily round, the common task
Will furnish all I need to ask.'

[*She takes the tray away then returns. She tries to get the crumbs off the cloth without removing it, puckering the cloth and dragging it to one side of the table. She finally manages it and with one hand full of crumbs triumphantly goes to the sideboard. She stops.*]

Where's the wastepaper basket?

[*Carefully maintaining the handful of crumbs, she looks under the sideboard and beside and under other furniture.*]

Where the hell's it gone? Alan!

[*She listens: no reply.*]

Alan!

[*Again no reply.*]

Fallen down deaf-mute with the palsy, I suppose.

[*She looks at the handful of crumbs and considers, then dumps them back on the tablecloth. She goes to the door.*]

Alan! What are you doing in that lavatory? I'll rephrase that. Alan, it is time you were out of the lavatory.

[*She listens.*]

You heard. Just get out of there and get into bed. Now.

[*She surveys the room again. She picks up coloured bricks and puts them into a tall cardboard box and clears other items similarly. Finally there is an elderly soft toy. She looks at it and adjusts its raggedy clothing.*]

What do you see with your one eye? Apart from a
windmill and a card saying normal service will be
resumed. And who knows, maybe it will. You only need
one eye to see hope if the sun's shining.
[*She goes to the door and calls.*]
If you're not out of there in the next twenty seconds I
shall come up and slap your bottom.
[*She listens.*]
I don't care if it might wake your sister!
[*to herself*] Thoughtful of you to mention it, though.
[*loud*] One, two, three . . .
[*She continues to count aloud as she crosses to the box and drops
a toy in. She lifts the box and carries it out. Behind the
box is the wastepaper basket. In due course she returns, still
counting. At '17, 18,' there is an audible slam, the sound of
feet scampering across the landing and another slam.*
JUDITH *looks in the appropriate direction.*]
Well, at least he recognizes numbers. Education has to
be improving. His father only recognizes figures.
[*She spots the wastepaper basket.*]
Wouldn't you know.
[*She empties the cloth into it then re-lays the cloth and puts the
basket where it should have been.*]
Now. Do the carrots. Oh to hell with it. Tin of peas.
[*The front door shuts, off.* JUDITH *looks at her watch with a
touch of surprise.*]
Ah. He's here.
[RICHARD *enters. The dialogue that follows is not continuous:
sometimes they are silent and sometimes they are doing things
during or between speaking.*]

RICHARD: Love.
JUDITH: Dick, dear. Good day?
RICHARD: Oh, you know.
JUDITH: Better than usual or worse than usual?
RICHARD: Somewhere between the two.
JUDITH: Exactly as usual.
RICHARD: Well no, not really.
JUDITH: No, I didn't think so.
RICHARD: You know how it is. The train was late. And it was

packed. I didn't get a seat until Preston Road. Then there was some woman jabbing her umbrella into me the rest of the way. Sometimes I think women ought to need licences to carry an umbrella.

JUDITH: Yes, dear.

RICHARD: Not all of them, of course. But you know what I mean.

JUDITH: Yes, Richard. You mean in the same way as men who practise off-drives in the dining room.

RICHARD: That was only once.

JUDITH: We only had one cut-glass fruit bowl. Once.

RICHARD: Are you trying to take me down a peg, or something?

JUDITH: Keeping my end up.

RICHARD: That's my girl.

[*He pats her playfully.*]

JUDITH: I thought you had the car in Holborn from yesterday.

RICHARD: Yes, but I had to leave it in town again. There are some heavy samples to be loaded into it tomorrow. They can do it before I get there. Saves time.

JUDITH: Not if your train's late in the morning, it won't. They'll all be standing there with dropped arches and double hernias, wondering where you got to at half-past-ten.

RICHARD: Look on the bright side. I shall be a damn' sight earlier than twenty-past-ten, anyway.

JUDITH: Half-past.

RICHARD: Heavens, I could walk it sooner than that.

JUDITH: Who's doing the loading? Not that little Lynn?

RICHARD: No, no. What about a sherry?

JUDITH: On a Tuesday?

RICHARD: Why not? Don't have to keep to a rigid pattern. Let's kick over the traces.

JUDITH: So long as you think we can afford it. Don't forget we've got Dad coming over on Sunday.

RICHARD: We'll manage. He always brings a bottle of duty-free.

JUDITH: Yes, but not sherry.

[*She gets the sherry.*]

Richard. If Lynn isn't doing the loading, who is?

RICHARD: Why?

JUDITH: You're not making Mrs. Brancaster do it?

RICHARD: No, of course not.

JUDITH: Thirty-four years of servants in South Africa and then another ten sitting on a rubber ring in Holborn Viaduct. The poor woman would never recover. She'd have to resign from the Trefoil Guild.

RICHARD: No. She wouldn't unload anything. It's as much as I can do to get her to change the office carbon paper.

JUDITH: Doesn't like the black on her fingers, I daresay.

RICHARD: I've taken on a young lad.

JUDITH: Has something happened in the wholesale paper trade that I don't know about? Sherry on a weekday, taking on a young lad.

RICHARD: I won't be paying him that much. It's time to open up a bit. Take a chance. I'm fairly sure I'm going to get the local council account. That's a lot of paper. And staples. And office clasps.

JUDITH: Office clasps?

RICHARD: They're a little metal thing we supply. For unstapling papers you've stapled together. They're busy people, these local council folk.

JUDITH: Well done, darling, that's tremendous.

RICHARD: Your father's not the only one who can do it, you see.

JUDITH: Dinner ought to be ready. You going upstairs?

RICHARD: Yes. Have they been good?

JUDITH: [*going*] Tolerable, I suppose. I wonder why we always say six is such a lovely age or four is such a lovely age. I think it may be that if we say it often enough we hope we'll come to believe it.
            [*She exits.*]

RICHARD: How can you say that about your own children, Judith? They're marvellous.

JUDITH: [*off*] You don't have them all day.

RICHARD: I wish I did.

JUDITH: [*off*] You don't have them all week. You only see them on Saturdays and Sundays. And then you're off playing a match.

RICHARD: I see them every morning.

JUDITH: [*putting her head round the door*] Yes. And you grunt at them. If you were their source of vocabulary they'd grow up monosyllabic.

[*She disappears again.*]

RICHARD: They could always pretend they came from Yorkshire. Good folk, Yorkshire folk. Guaranteed to disappoint. Right.

[*He finishes his sherry.* JUDITH *re-enters.*]

JUDITH: Don't be long.

RICHARD: Just give 'em a quick kiss and wash my hands.

JUDITH: It's shepherd's pie.

RICHARD: We had that yesterday.

JUDITH: That was hot-pot.

RICHARD: What's the difference?

JUDITH: Shepherd's pie is drier. That's why you get it next day.

RICHARD: [*going*] You going to make some gravy, then?

[JUDITH *looks blankly at him as he goes. She sighs.*]

JUDITH: Gravy now. It'll be candles on the grand piano next. If we had a grand piano. [*checks*] Salt, pepper, water, glasses. Tomato sauce! [*calls*] I take it you want ketchup as well as gravy.

RICHARD: [*off*] What, dear?

JUDITH: You heard.

RICHARD: [*off*] You're going to make gravy?

JUDITH: I'm going to make gravy.

RICHARD: [*off*] Lovely.

[*Pause.*]

JUDITH: D'you want tomato sauce as well?

RICHARD: [*off*] Rather. Only live once.

JUDITH: [*to herself*] I don't know why I bother to ask.

[*She goes off humming, half-singing 'When the Country Gardens Come to Town' and returns with the ketchup bottle. She sets it down and sits, looking towards the door. She fiddles with the place settings in silence. Eventually* RICHARD *reappears.*]

How did you get the local council order, darling? I thought you said they'd had the same supplier since way back, before the War, in the thirties, and they wouldn't look at anybody else.

RICHARD: I haven't actually got the order yet.

JUDITH: Oh, I see. Weren't we rather cracking the bottle before it was labelled, then?

RICHARD: No, but I've as good as got it.

JUDITH: You sure, pet? This isn't going to be another big disappointment later, like Clerkenwell Road?

RICHARD: Clerkenwell Road was quite different. You know very well why I missed out there.

JUDITH: Yes, I do.

RICHARD: This isn't the same at all. It's not remotely similar.

JUDITH: I see.

RICHARD: Not remotely.

JUDITH: Then?

RICHARD: The chap who always supplied them is retiring.

JUDITH: Well, that doesn't mean you'll get it.

RICHARD: He's recommending me. He's closing his company down and putting them on to me.

JUDITH: That's very good of him. Does he ride a donkey?

RICHARD: What the hell does that mean?

JUDITH: Your rivals don't usually give you their business. Nobody's rivals do.

RICHARD: Well, he is.

JUDITH: Uncommonly nice of him. Do you know him through the horticultural, or do you see him on the train or something?

RICHARD: No, no. It's Lynn's father, actually.

JUDITH: Oh.

RICHARD: He's probably trying to make sure there's a job for his daughter after he's retired.

JUDITH: How strategic.

          [RICHARD *looks at her.*]

RICHARD: You have a good day?

JUDITH: I rang the television repair man.

RICHARD: Oh, I'd forgotten. Damn it.

JUDITH: And when Alan came in from school I took them both to the park, you know, the one past the cemetery and the flats with the green roofs. They were fairly exhausted by the time we got there. Thought that might be a good thing. Then we found the pond was empty. I think emptying the pond must be somebody's full-time job. So we sat and looked at the concrete. Then Alan got shouted at by the keeper because he decided he wanted to prove he could walk on concrete. After that we went to the playground. Lucy fell over in the sandpit, a sadly wet area of the sandpit for which I don't think she was personally responsible. The pond was dry, the sandpit was wet. And poor Lucy's knickers were like emery paper. So she cried, and I sat on a swing and then I caught Alan playing some dreadful game of flicking nose-bogies with that Derek Hare boy, then the keeper shouted at me for sitting on a swing where only sub-pubertoids may rest.

RICHARD: I don't suppose it was that bad.

JUDITH: We did manage to drag ourselves home afterwards. It was two very crotchety infants that went to bed. They were so tired of course they didn't want to go to bed.

RICHARD: They were fine when I was up there. Fresh rounded little things all tousled in the sheets. They're at a lovely age.

JUDITH: I believe it.

RICHARD: When's he coming?

JUDITH: Who?

RICHARD: The man.

JUDITH: What man?

RICHARD: The repair man. For the television.

JUDITH: Thursday, at ten.

RICHARD: Ah. You must be sure to be in.

JUDITH: I'll be in.

RICHARD: I'm in Wapping on Thursday. Wapping on Thursday, Northampton on Friday.

JUDITH: Northampton?

RICHARD: Chasing another account. These days you've got to hunt the business up — even if it does mean going further afield. That's what your father says, isn't it?

JUDITH: I think he says hunt it down. Seems more likely. Though I'm not sure it's a good way of looking at things.

[*The telephone rings.* JUDITH *answers it.*]

Byron 8862. Just a moment.

[*She hands the phone to* RICHARD.]

RICHARD: Hello. Oh, hello.

[JUDITH *looks at him.* RICHARD *gives her a deprecating wave as if to indicate that he can handle it and she can go.*]

Well, about to have dinner, actually —— Yes, of course
it was ——
> [*There is a fair amount of eye contact between* JUDITH *and*
> RICHARD *during this.*]

I don't know why you should have thought that —— So,
what can I do for you? —— [*emphasized, to indicate*
JUDITH *is still here*] Yes, yes —— When would you like me
to bring the samples over? —— Oh, any day.
> [JUDITH *gives him a particular look.*]

Friday, yes, but what about tomorrow? —— Why don't
I give you a ring in the morning to confirm the time?
Unfortunately my diary's still in the office —— Thanks
so much, I look forward to that.
> [*He puts down the receiver.*]

JUDITH: Business hunting you up?

RICHARD: That's it.

JUDITH: Or are you hunting it, up?

RICHARD: You've got to try and keep ahead.

JUDITH: You certainly have.

RICHARD: [*determinedly trying to lighten the tone.*] Homes like this don't
grow on trees.

JUDITH: Oh, I don't know. Most of the furniture did. Except
for the formica top.
> [*No response.*]

And maybe some of the inhabitants.
> [*Short pause.*]

RICHARD: [*sharply*] Are you going to get dinner?

JUDITH: I'm not sure.
> [*She looks at him and goes.*]

RICHARD: [*calls*] What are you upset about now?
> [*No response. He goes to the door.*]

What's all this about?

JUDITH: [*off*] You tell me.

RICHARD: Why are you going off in a tantrum?
> [*Pause.* JUDITH *returns.*]

JUDITH: How long has our number been on the office stationery?

RICHARD: It isn't. Oh darling, don't tell me you've lost your
head because a client rather desperately needs some
supplies.

JUDITH: My head's still firmly on my shoulders. That's one of my strong points, Richard. Your client, however, must certainly have been desperate to ring you at home at seven-forty in the evening. Especially as she needs you to bring samples. I would have thought if she was truly desperate she would have known what she wanted.

RICHARD: She does.

JUDITH: Yes, I bet she does.

RICHARD: There are different weights and qualities and prices.

JUDITH: If she knows what she wants she could simply order it, I would have thought, without further calls and visits. Do only your women customers have the number, by the way?

RICHARD: Calm down, for Christ's sake. She's just the girl from a drawing office down by Seven Dials and, if you want the boring details, what she wants is some Chinese octavo cartridge at fifty pounds. Because of Chairman Mao we can't get the Chinese import any more and I don't have any fifty pound in stock in the quality she would need. So I've got to find her some suitable alternative. That's business, Judith. That's trade. That's what I have to spend my bloody day doing while you suffer the agonies of playing with the children in a sandpit. And don't think I wouldn't swop!

  [*A long pause.*]

JUDITH: I was being silly. It's consommé to start.

  [*She goes.* RICHARD *sits down.* JUDITH *returns with soups and they sip them.*]

  Sorry, darling. But you have done it before.

RICHARD: Forget it.

  [*They continue with their soup.*]

  Any news of the bridge?

JUDITH: They're replacing it.

RICHARD: Well, I know that. But are they closing the line down?

JUDITH: Only overnight, apparently.

RICHARD: I don't see how that's going to work.

JUDITH: Well, according to Miss Epstein in the post office, you know the thin one with the pince-nez? Keeps her cat on the counter.

RICHARD: That post office.

JUDITH: The one near the station. Well, according to her it'll all take several weeks —

RICHARD: That's what I thought.

JUDITH: But they'll build a complete new bridge alongside, only it's all on rollers. The old bridge keeps going as usual, the trains run over it as though nothing's happening. They're just not affected. Then at the last minute, when the new bridge is fully constructed, they roll the old one away and it's held by a scaffolding-derrick affair, and the new one is rolled in in its place. They just have to re-lay the track where it joins, and dismantle the old bridge sufficiently to transport it away. Very clever.

RICHARD: Sounds smart.

JUDITH: And she says they do that overnight. She told me the date, but I've forgotten it. The last train out of town will be about seven, and once it's through they'll close the line and work through the night. Of course, they'll have to close the road underneath it as well. The traffic will have to go along Pinner Road and round, I suppose. And everything's ready to start again at six o'clock next morning. Apparently.

RICHARD: Very sharp. Must have taken some planning.

JUDITH: Yes.

>   [*Pause.*]

>   How did that girl have our number?

RICHARD: I don't know. Lynn may have given it to her. They're old friends. That's probably it.

JUDITH: Lynn?

RICHARD: Er, yes.

JUDITH: Finished?

RICHARD: I think so.

>   [JUDITH *stands holding the plates.*]

JUDITH: It's very good of Lynn's father, isn't it?

RICHARD: Yes it is, though as you said, we must wait and see. It's this Sunday John is coming, is it?

JUDITH: Father?

RICHARD: Do we know any other Johns?

JUDITH: Several.

RICHARD: Oh.

JUDITH: Yes, he's coming on Sunday. Only to lunch, though. It's Mum's birthday next week so he'll be going over with some flowers in the afternoon.

RICHARD: She would have been 61 this year.

JUDITH: Sixty. No, you're right, she'd have been 61.

RICHARD: He'll have his car?

JUDITH: Oh yes.

RICHARD: And Lilian?

JUDITH: Aunt Lilian hasn't come with him for ages. Not since we had outside done. And she never comes when he's going to the cemetery. Says it upsets her too much: walking on all that gravel with her hip.

[*She leaves with the plates.*]

RICHARD: He won't need a lift, then.

[*While* JUDITH *is out,* RICHARD *finds his diary in his briefcase and starts looking through it.* JUDITH *returns with the gravy. She takes in what he is doing before she puts it down.*]

RICHARD: When's Alan's half-term?

JUDITH: I'm not sure. Not till next month.

RICHARD: They get a week these days, don't they?

JUDITH: I think it's been a week for years.

RICHARD: Hm. I was wondering, perhaps you'd like to take the kids away for it, have a bit of a break.

JUDITH: And leave you? Working?

RICHARD: I couldn't get away, that's for sure.

JUDITH: No.

RICHARD: But don't worry about that. No reason why you shouldn't get down to the sea, have some sea air.

JUDITH: A bit expensive.

RICHARD: Out of season.

JUDITH: What about you?

RICHARD: I'll just have to manage. I'd be happy enough that you were all away having a little holiday.

JUDITH: Yes.

RICHARD: What do you say?

JUDITH: I say: if Lynn isn't doing the loading, and Mrs. Brancaster isn't doing the loading, the young lad will have to wait

for you anyway, because he won't be able to lift those
heavy rolls on his own. So what's the point of leaving the
car? In Holborn, overnight.
[*Pause.*]

RICHARD: What's your game?

JUDITH: It's not my game, Richard. The car isn't in Holborn,
is it?

RICHARD: God, this is like the Bloody Assizes. Of course it's
in Holborn. In the car park, behind the stores.

JUDITH: It's not any kind of assize. It's a family, it's a marriage.
Or it was.

RICHARD: Well, if the marriage is in the past tense, remember
it takes two to break it. Don't put it all on me.

JUDITH: It usually takes three to break it. At least.
[*A long silence.*]
Aren't you going to say anything?

RICHARD: I don't know what to say. I'm entirely at a loss.

JUDITH: I want you to say the truth, because I can't go on like
this.

RICHARD: Like what? I offer you a holiday. Business begins to
look up and I want my family to be the first to benefit.

JUDITH: And you check the dates in a diary you left in the office.

RICHARD: This isn't the office diary.

JUDITH: Then why does it say it is, on the cover?
[*Silence.* RICHARD *puts the diary on the table, front cover
downwards.*]

JUDITH: You wanted us out of the way.

RICHARD: Don't be stupid.

JUDITH: Treat me as a human being! Because I care!
[*Short silence.*]
After eight years of marriage, three affairs that I know of,
you generously offer your wife and two children a week
at Lyme Regis or Brighton when the funfair will be
closed and the sea will be breaking on the promenade,
lashed by winds that will carry their kiss-me-quick hats
and spun-sugar-fungus-on-a-stick forty miles inland.
[*very still*] I'm grateful.
[*Pause.*]

RICHARD: I need the time.

JUDITH: [*almost a whisper*] Thank you.

RICHARD: It'll sort out.

JUDITH: One way or another.

RICHARD: I spend a lot of time away trying to get new accounts, stuck in hotels and guest houses. It's not much fun. And what can you do at night? Go to the pub, go to the bar, go to a restaurant. It's boring, lonely. No shape to it.

JUDITH: It's not exactly a *fête champêtre* down here.

RICHARD: No, but you got the kids, you got home, you got the neighbours, things around you, things you can do. Even when they irritate you, they're there. A Gideon's Bible and a Teasmade are pretty limited company.

JUDITH: Surely.

RICHARD: And it's depressing. Just got wall-to-wall carpets down at home here, and you find yourself back on lino. Notices in the bathroom. No fridge. So. You try to make some friends. People the landscape. It's quite natural.

JUDITH: Oh yes.

RICHARD: Then sometimes, not always, mind, just occasionally, things get out of hand.

JUDITH: Yes.

RICHARD: I'm not an evil person, you know.

JUDITH: Richard, I love you.

RICHARD: I know, I know. But it's not easy.
   [*Brief pause.*]

JUDITH: We could talk on the phone more often, if you have to be away.

RICHARD: Do you know how bleak it is when you've been talking to home and hearing the news, and the music in the background, and the kids, and then you're back in your room and it's dead silent and all you've got's the flowered wallpaper to stare at? It's usually bloody pink.
   [*Pause.*]

JUDITH: Why do it? We could live on less. Let's go back to lino. I don't care. It's you I married, not Cyril Lord.

RICHARD: Oh no. I want a nice home. Don't want your father always offering us things to make it better because it doesn't measure up to his standards.

JUDITH: He means it kindly. He's only got us.

RICHARD: I'm the breadwinner.

JUDITH: I hope so.

> [*Pause.*]

How deeply in are you?

RICHARD: Deep.

> [JUDITH *nods.* RICHARD *looks at her.*]

I'd better start sorting things out.

> [JUDITH *looks at him.*]

I can't do it in front of you. Not with you here.

JUDITH: I'll turn the gas off then.

> [*She goes to the door.*]

When you've sorted it out . . . ?

RICHARD: I don't know. I don't know.

JUDITH: I see. I'll be in the garden. Weeding.

RICHARD: It's dark.

JUDITH: So much the better.

> [*She goes.* RICHARD *sits for a moment or two, takes off his jacket, goes to the phone and dials three letters and four figures.*]

RICHARD: Margaret? —— Yes, of course it is, darling. Your call earlier rather put the feline in the aviary —— Yes, of course she was —— Well, I had to do something, didn't I? Civilized behaviour and all that —— No, she's gone out now. The thing is this, I've been thinking, you know what I was saying the other night, well, I've made up my mind. It's not fair that I go on like this; it's not fair to Judith and above all it's not fair to you. So I've made up my mind. I've told Judith it's over —— Yes, we're splitting —— Well, I don't know, I mean, she wasn't pleased —— It's such a relief, it means we can be together, darling. God, it's what I've always wanted since I first saw you. What? —— No, I don't think so, that'll have to be arranged, but no, they'd stay with her. I'll have access, I suppose, but let's face it, they'd rather cramp your style. Hell, I can't wait! —— Mm? What, darling? ——

> [*He listens for a considerable time.*]

How do you mean? —— But I love you —— Well, I know she does, but that's over —— Come on, Meg, this isn't my girl with the skin like golden velvet. You're perfection, you know that? —— You don't mean that. Meg, you don't mean that ——— I'm giving up my family. Do you think Lucy and Alan don't mean anything to me? ——— Yes, and eight years of marriage and everything I've put into this house ——— I see. Well, why do you think I said what I said the other night? ——— Of course I meant it. I thought we were all lined up——— Ah, go jump off a bridge! ——— Yes, well, I've got feelings too ——— Go to hell!

> [*He rings off. He gets up and paces slowly. He takes out his wallet and removes a photograph, puts a match to it and places it on a side plate. (The water jug is handy if needed.) He takes his diary and throws it in his briefcase. He stands looking.* JUDITH *appears in the doorway. After a moment she speaks.*]

JUDITH: Finished?

> [RICHARD *turns and nods.*]

I thought so. Saw you moving about.

> [*Pause.*]

Is it over?

> [RICHARD *looks at her and nods his head.*]

Between us, I mean.

> [*He again nods his head.*]

You mean . . . ?

RICHARD: Do you think I was going to throw all this away?

JUDITH: I'm not sure I can take this.

RICHARD: I don't deserve it, I know. And you don't deserve what I hand out to you. I'm sorry, Jude. I do the best I can, you know. I suppose it's being a man; I've got to prove it and all that, Jack the lad. But in the end, your heart is where your home is. If this wasn't the one that mattered, I wouldn't be here, would I? This is where I always come back.

JUDITH: Not if you're going to go again later.

RICHARD: I've told her, Judith. There won't be any more. Not now. Not ever. Time I grew up.

JUDITH: I won't go on as a pillow-cum-punchbag. I can't.

RICHARD: You don't want me? I don't blame you.

JUDITH: I do. But all of you. Not just the bits you can spare.

> [*She turns away. In silence* RICHARD *kneels and looks at her.*]

No.

RICHARD: I can't get any lower. I need you.

                    [*Pause.*]
JUDITH: I was so sure you were going. This time I was sure.
RICHARD: Going just isn't a possibility. Not when you face it
           square on. Let me stay. I want to stay. With you.
JUDITH: Do you really mean it?
RICHARD: I'm a fool, darling, but I'm not that daft.
                    [*He gets up.*]
           When you've got the best son, the best daughter and the
           best missus in the world, you don't chuck them away for
           some little sexpot with no depth to her.
JUDITH: It's for keeps, though, isn't it?
RICHARD: Of course.
JUDITH: I was quite certain you were just going to ring Lynn
           and say you were on your way over to her. I really knew
           this was going to be it.
RICHARD: Wasn't Lynn!
JUDITH: No?
RICHARD: No, no, no. Was a girl called Margaret. Lynn!
JUDITH: I thought that was why her father . . .
RICHARD: Suspicious cow! No, he's retiring like I told you. But
           I wanted to ring Margaret and finish it properly. Clean
           slate and all that.
JUDITH: Margaret. I hope she wasn't too broken up.
RICHARD: She'll pull through, I think.
JUDITH: Richard. I love you.
RICHARD: I love you. I'll have to go and get the car sometime,
           though.
JUDITH: Where is it really?
RICHARD: Hebden Bridge.
JUDITH: Hebden Bridge! That's Yorkshire!
RICHARD: I know. I was batting up there so hard it blew a gasket.
           I had to leave it at a garage.
JUDITH: That's where you and she . . . ?
RICHARD: Yes. We could all go up at the weekend. There's a
           smashing place there, the White Lion.
JUDITH: Not if that's where you stayed with her.
RICHARD: Perhaps not.
                    [*They look at each other and smile.*]
JUDITH: The shepherd's pie will be wrecked.

RICHARD: Who cares?

JUDITH: You've got to eat something.

RICHARD: So have you.

JUDITH: I don't think I could. My stomach feels like the North Sea.

RICHARD: Yeah.

[*He pats her bum.*]

JUDITH: I'll go down the road and get some fish and chips.

RICHARD: I can go.

JUDITH: You're not going anywhere. You just stay here. Back in a mo'.

[*She goes.* RICHARD *pours himself a glass of water and drinks one or two mouthfuls. The telephone starts to ring. He goes to it, lifts the receiver and replaces it; then he leaves it off. We hear the tone. He returns to the water. The lights fade. Then the sound fades.*]

END OF ACT ONE

ACT TWO

Letting Go

SCENE ONE

A room in JOHN HOCKADAY's *house. Items of furniture and personal memorabilia are about.* JUDITH, *now about fifty, is there alone.*

JUDITH: Funny to think this place will be empty now. At least it won't be. But he won't be coming back. None of us. Not now. So full of his past, all our pasts. This was their dream. This is what they built between them, the inside show. Dad in his uniform, Squadron Leader Hockaday, Bomber Command. 'Hock' to his friends, despite the German connotation. I don't remember him much then: a shadowy figure, pale blue, who firmed up later in a darker uniform with more rings round the sleeves and more time to spare.

Part of my life's here too. The concrete surround of the downpipe drain where I fell off my tricycle and gashed my knee. It's still there. And the scar on my leg. The corner round behind the coalshed where I used to play shops with Nigel. Ha! I set off on my bike from here with Hugh, that time he tried to put his hand down my knickers. And let's face it, it's from here we set off those times I let him put his hand down them. Asked him to.

Strange to think those very guilty experiences were — truly — innocent. And joyous. I don't think I've ever had an experience quite so thrilling, surprising or exciting — oh dear — as those early ones, held in quotation marks by rides on my Hercules tourer. Except I suppose having the children, but that wasn't the act, it was the fulfilment. Yes, they were the best.

Funny to think this house means that to me. Mum and Dad, I cheerfully hope, never thought that happened here. We were confident it had never happened between them: we were just miracles. And they behaved as if it never crossed their minds that it might happen with us.

Sad now. Empty. Wound-down clocks. No noise, no smells, no cisterns filling. The Indian carpet, brought home by BEA who I'm sure were unaware of the courtesy. Worn well. Always had an eye for quality, Dad. That awful table from his parents' place. A home is a jigsaw really. Bit by bit, things are gathered together, manifestations of need and momentary wealth, of taste, of friendships, of time spent in this place or that — the sugar spoon from Sidmouth, the rattan chair from Kuching — and the marks: the chips, the stains, the hasty repaint voicelessly witness a history. And a picture emerges only at the very end. A picture of a life, just one family. At the time they don't much signify: objects, functions. When the lives they served are filleted out these things fossilize their route. Marker-buoys. Very potent. And they gather dust to make anyone weep.

Don't go, Dad. I'm not ready. I wish to God you could be here. You are right in this place. The things you did to it, the extension, the double glazing. You took pleasure in the things you did, your skills, your rotten bricklaying. It was yours. It is yours. And the great building of the bothy. Like Babel, the air was filled with language. You managed it though before our teenage years were entirely over. It saved us a lot of bike rides. Friday night was heavy petting night. Not to any great effect, I remember; except with Peter who disliked wearing underpants, which made the topography of his trousers more interesting. And Gillian used to sit up there practising the recorder, practising the violin. That building spared a lot of people. You were so proud of it.

And Christmases here. The uncles and sweet, proper, dreary Aunt Lilian. Eking out an emotional life on the basis of her one true beau, buried at the Somme, and what might have been. Poor old Aunt Lilian. And us giving them 'Chanson de Matin' and whatever that wretched thing was I used to call 'Lebensraum'. And mother's monumental Christmas lunches, as she got thinner. Waste and waste.

When she died I was pleased she was out of the suffering. And I'll be pleased when . . . I don't wish it. But there's a difference. When Mum died we were all energized because we'd got to keep ourselves together. Somehow we gloried her by pushing on. Remembering her, oh shit, we remembered her, but pushing on. When you go, that cobweb of shared experience, that concatenation of lives will be taken apart, limb by limb, strand by strand, very swiftly. The house will go drab, the weeds will grow; but in a few months there'll be an exchange of contracts and somebody fresh and budding with life, probably with kids with sticky fingers, will come hurtling in here and see just how they can improve it all. They'll cover up the paper you brought back when you were on the Amsterdam run; they'll paint over the gold leaf on the bosses; get a smarter fridge; the carpets will be other colours and slowly, swiftly, the garden will grow to a different shape, paths will lead to different places, the hedge will be grubbed up or sprout to ten feet tall. And a year or two from now we'll look at it — I'll look at it — and say, was this the place where I grew to consciousness, our place? What happened to the love you put in?

What happened was it fetched ninety-five. That was the price of it. And in a few years more someone else's loving care or utter disinterest will fetch more. Well.

No, don't go yet, Dad. I'm not ready for the white-out, wipe-out, Whitsun ending.

SCENE TWO

A private room in a nursing home or hospital. JOHN HOCKADAY, *old
and near to death, is lying in bed.* JUDITH, *his daughter, no doubt
bearing an appropriate gift, comes in.*

JOHN: Like a waking dream from childhood, lying here. It
           can't be true, but it is.
JUDITH: How are you?
JOHN: Don't ask.
JUDITH: Is it . . . is it getting worse?
JOHN: How do you measure pain? Its frequency? Acuteness?
           How much it blots out all other thought?
JUDITH: So sorry, Dad.
JOHN: I'm not your father.
JUDITH: You are, Dad.
JOHN: Am I? How strange. I don't remember that.
JUDITH: I'm Judith.
JOHN: Judith? You're Elisabeth. Why d'you call yourself
           Judith?
JUDITH: You gave me the name.
JOHN: They all say that.
JUDITH: Mummy died. Elisabeth. Cancer, don't you remember?
           You had to cancel the holiday hotel.
JOHN: When was that?
JUDITH: Oh, a long while ago.
           [*Pause.*]
JOHN: Why did no one tell me? I should have been told.
JUDITH: They did, they did. You've forgotten.
JOHN: I couldn't forget if Elisabeth died. She's my darling.
JUDITH: [*matter-of-factly*] And she was my Mum.
JOHN: Was she now? Fancy. She never told me that. Did I ever
           tell you about the time we went down Peddars Way?
JUDITH: You and Mum?
JOHN: Elisabeth and me, yes.
JUDITH: I don't think so.
JOHN: We walked. It was very hot. I remember that. One of
           those singeing Norfolk late summer days. Very hot,
           very still.

JUDITH: Yes?

JOHN: What do you mean, 'yes'?

JUDITH: What happened?

JOHN: Nothing happened. We went for a walk. Isn't that enough? It was pleasant. Blackberries and Michaelmas daisies.

JUDITH: Are they looking after you all right?

JOHN: Who?

JUDITH: The nurses.

JOHN: I don't know, dear, you'd better ask them.

JUDITH: I'm sure they are. Is the food all right?

JOHN: I don't take very much food, my dear. I never had much of an appetite, you know.

JUDITH: You bugger, you used to eat like a horse.

JOHN: I can be content with very little. In the food department. Have you come a long way?

JUDITH: Just from North Harrow.

JOHN: North Harrow. Oh yes, I remember North Harrow, I went to the Embassy there.

JUDITH: No darling, I don't think that would have been North Harrow. Um. I don't know. It might have been Knightsbridge, St. John's Wood, somewhere like that.

JOHN: No. Embassy in Knightsbridge? No, no. It was North Harrow.

JUDITH: No darling, I don't think so, not an Embassy in North Harrow.

JOHN: I saw 'The Small Back Room' there. And 'The Third Man'.

JUDITH: Oh, a cinema.

JOHN: Or was that the Langham . . . ?

JUDITH: I didn't realize you meant a cinema . . .

JOHN: That's what I said, the Embassy.

JUDITH: It's not there now.

JOHN: Nothing much is these days.

[Pause.]

That's the terror. You lose your points of reference. It's not that the lamplighters are retired and gone, it's that they've moved the lamp-posts, changed the whole bloody system. Teachers, relatives, everyone you grew up with, entertainers, politicians — I don't mind so much about them — your heroes, and society people who made scandals, fade away as though they'd never been. And you're left holding dust, tasting dust, that once was the fabric of your world. You wonder where it went, what your bearings are now. And there's no one to ask. They all think you're simple.

JUDITH: I've felt the first chill of it, even at my age.

JOHN: Did you ever see Blaney and Farrar?

[JUDITH *shakes her head.*]

Lilian used to like them, till one of them got married. I don't know who they are now.

[*Pause.*]

Siren-suits, horsedrawn trams; people smile when you mention them.

[JUDITH *nods and smiles.*]

They belong in the ark. They're part of my living experience. My life is invested in them. It's unnerving to find what you think immediate, tangible, consigned in your presence to meaninglessness. Makes a man nervy.

[JUDITH *takes his hand.*]

JUDITH: You did plenty of the consigning, at the joystick of the Wellington, the Brabazon, the Avro-York.

JOHN: Knew where the lamp-posts were then. And the fires. Can I have some water?

JUDITH: I'll pour you some from the jug here. There you are. Would you like me to hold it?

JOHN: Hold my head. It falls about a lot these days. Spring's gone.

[JUDITH *helps him drink.*]

JUDITH: [*looking through the window*] Lovely view. ·

JOHN: Can't see it.

JUDITH: Can't you?

JOHN: The light hurts.

JUDITH: It's a lovely view. A field that dips away. Couple of oaks and some chestnuts. Lots of birds in the trees.

JOHN: Rooks.

JUDITH: I thought you couldn't see.

JOHN: I hear them. When they gather.

JUDITH: There are other birds, too. Sparrows, blackbirds, starlings, lots of starlings.

JOHN: Where's Richard?

JUDITH: Richard?

JOHN: You're Judith, aren't you?

JUDITH: Yes.

JOHN: Where's Richard?

JUDITH: Richard left me a long time ago.

JOHN: I'm sorry.

JUDITH: Years ago. You were a brick at the time.

JOHN: Yes.

JUDITH: Just before you stopped flying.

JOHN: Why don't I remember?

JUDITH: You took some leave to help me with the children. And with me.

[JOHN *looks uncomprehendingly at her.*]

Richard set up with a girl from his office whose father was helping him with business. Lynn. She was younger than me. Slimmer hips. A genuine brunette. Under it all.

JOHN: Poor woman.

JUDITH: He's not with her now. [*smiles*] I was better out of it. And the children were less confused.

JOHN: Everything's just library books, you know. They all go back. Whether it's the furniture or a working body with arms and legs, they go. Even the things you think you've achieved, the things you worked for, they get forgotten, filed under oblivion before you've finished your bacon and eggs. There's only here and now, and it doesn't bloody last!

JUDITH: Don't be angry.

JOHN: I'm the me that was a boy, still!

JUDITH: Yes.

JOHN: And I can't do it. Dressed in a corpse.

JUDITH: Relax, please.

JOHN: Oh no. No, no. Don't try and avoid anger, suppress it, deny it, get rid of it. Anger's vital, it's the centre of the universe. The earth was made from fire, shaped by the violence of ice and volcano. Anger is just raw energy, ready to tackle what comes and get on with it. Without it we'd be like flatfish, lying on the bottom with two eyes gawping upwards.

JUDITH: I wouldn't mistake you for that.

JOHN: Use it. Channel it, regulate it, aim and control it. But thank the stars for it. Anger's man's saving grace.

JUDITH: Acceptance comes into it, too.

JOHN: No.

[*Pause.*]

JUDITH: I gave a lift to one of Alan's friends on my way here; he wanted to come into town. As far as Finchley Road, anyway. And I looked at him when he was putting his seatbelt on and it suddenly struck me how beautiful he was, the smoothness of his flesh, unclouded eyes and lids that were soft and shaped, not flecked and drooping. Firm soft. Fresh. When I was younger I wouldn't have noticed him; I'd have been put off by the shape of his nose, or his haircut, or something. His choice of clothes. And I thought about Alan. He's . . . ordinary looking, bland still, unweathered. But the exuberance, the promise, the abundant head of hair. I think everyone under twenty-five is startling. And it pleases me. I'm not in there competing.

JOHN: You should be.

JUDITH: That would spoil it. I'm outside, enjoying them, knowing them — or not — seeing them whole and very happy with them, happy at them, as they are.

JOHN: Sounds as though you've given up.

JUDITH: Not at all. It's a privilege of middle age. A kind of respite. Maybe even a reward.

JOHN: I'm not going peacefully. Don't tell 'em I went peacefully. I'm not. I'm on stinging nettles to live.

JUDITH: Why can't it be easier?

JOHN: Because it can't. Never is. Death's agony, short or long.

JUDITH: Don't say that.

JOHN: It's the truth. [*softens*] Rather like listening to one of your recorder recitals when you were a child. You and Gillie. Only it doesn't stop.

JUDITH: Our recorder recitals, I seem to remember, stopped rather frequently.

JOHN: It was their most attractive feature.

JUDITH: I promise I won't start playing now.

JOHN: If only you could. Then or now.

[*There is a long pause.* JUDITH *looks at him, then she remembers the small gift she has brought and looks in her bag for it. She finds it and puts it on the locker beside his bed.* JOHN *looks at her, his mind receding once again.*]

Did you come far?

JUDITH: Yes, darling, North Harrow. I told you.

JOHN: North Harrow.

JUDITH: Not far, really. Parked at Chalk Farm and came down on the tube.

JOHN: North Harrow.

JUDITH: Home, yes.

JOHN: I used to go to the pictures in North Harrow.

JUDITH: Yes, you said.

JOHN: Now what did I see there?

JUDITH: We've been over that, Dad. It's gone now, the cinema.

JOHN: Is it? Trouble with getting old. You are, you only are, what your mind retains you are.

JUDITH: There could be some advantages in that.

[JOHN *looks at her.*]

JOHN: You've been a good girl. Couldn't have married a better girl.

JUDITH: I'm Judith, Dad.

JOHN: Are you?

JUDITH: Yes, darling, you know I am.

JOHN: Always had such a good memory, good at maths, too. Richard left you, you say. Yes, I think I recall. What a loss. What a dead loss he was. Ah! It hurts.

JUDITH: Darling.

JOHN: Don't suppose anyone likes being hurt. All the same, I can't bear the thought of leaving. I want the singing to go on. Even the pain's a kind of moat. When you're edging along the way so many silly things matter. He got his promotion before me; your place is bigger than ours.

We always won on the foreign holidays, because of the airline. What pathetic victories. They don't matter. It's not only they don't matter. They're disgusting. They disgust me. Based on the error that this tiny fragment of time has importance. It's what we turn it into. It's the grace of our actions alone that can dignify this speck of eternity. And then only maybe. What matters is being. Then there's a chance. What matters is . . . I've been lucky, you know.

JUDITH: I'm not so sure. Mum's cancer, us to bring up on your own. Two world wars, all the friends you lost, pilots and crew, bright in their peak caps. All the killing you had to do, the destruction of your bombs. Was that really so lucky?

JOHN: Oh, I don't remember that. I suppose it must be lucky: I lived to tell the tale. Only I don't remember what the tale is. I know the feeling. And now I know the pain. Once there was a time . . .
    [*Pause.*]
Shall I tell you something? I have the most lovely daughter. Name's Judith. You must meet her sometime. You'd like her. It's very kind of you to come all this way. You know, people don't believe it when I tell them I'm ninety. One of the nurses — not — [*points*] — another one, sitting on my bed this morning, expect her legs were tired, and I said to her, 'D'you know I'm ninety?' And she said, 'I don't believe it.'

JUDITH: You're not ninety.

JOHN: What?

JUDITH: You aren't ninety.

JOHN: Aren't I?

JUDITH: No, darling. You were 79 in April.
    [*Pause.*]

JOHN: Who are you?

JUDITH: I'm Judith, your daughter.

JOHN: You must have put on weight, then. It comes again. Hold me.

JUDITH: Hang on to the good times. Governor of your old school, remember? Holidays in Norfolk, the bothy — remember when you built the bothy?

JOHN: No.

JUDITH: You did. You did it.

JOHN: I don't know.

JUDITH: I love you. I do love you.

JOHN: Hold me. Where am I going? What's the. . . ?

JUDITH: Mummy'll be there.

JOHN: She won't remember me.

JUDITH: She will.

JOHN: I'm afraid.

JUDITH: You can't be afraid. In the War, after the War, all those people's lives in your hands. You held me when I fell as a child and bled. Put your arms round me when. . . How would I have survived Richard's going if you hadn't given me the strength? You've got nothing to be afraid of. It's a victory for you, Dad.

JOHN: Where is everyone? Cuddle me. Cuddle me!

[*He dies.* JUDITH *holds him, lowers him gently, maybe screams in silence. She composes herself and stands up.*]

JUDITH: Nurse!

[*Blackout.*]

END OF ACT TWO

ACT THREE

Sands

> A beach in East Anglia. There is a ridge of stones, some bits and
> pieces that have been washed ashore, and to one side, a breakwater.
> It is summer in the middle of the Great War.
>
> LILIAN HOCKADAY, aged 17, and her brother JOHN, a couple of
> years younger, are just home from their respective boarding
> schools. They are the children of a medical practitioner in a
> nearby village. They enter.

LILIAN: Aren't we a little old for building sandcastles?

JOHN: I'm told some people do it all their lives.

LILIAN: We are not some people. We're Hockadays.

JOHN: I know that.

LILIAN: Well then. What if some of the village children saw us?
We'd never live it down.

JOHN: They haven't broken up yet; they're still at school.

LILIAN: Getting in the harvest, more likely. Some of their
parents have no morals. Interrupt their children's
education without a thought.

JOHN: I expect it's because so many of the men are away.

LILIAN: No, it's always been the same. I can remember.

JOHN: It'll have to be cricket, then.

LILIAN: That's all right. I'm much better at cricket than you are.

JOHN: No bowling underarm.

LILIAN: Why not?

JOHN: It's not allowed. God, girls are cissy. I can't think what
anybody sees in them.

LILIAN: You're asking to get your ears boxed, young man.

JOHN: 'You're asking to get your ears boxed, young man.'

LILIAN: Underarm bowling, for your information, is part of the
rules of cricket. That's how it began. Dr. Grace regularly
played —

JOHN: — In the Middle Ages overarm bowling was widespread.
There are pictures of it in galleries all over the world.

LILIAN: Are there?

JOHN: See, you don't know. Just shows how ignorant you are.
[*Pause.*]

LILIAN: I don't know what the King Henry School does for other boys; it seems to be achieving remarkably little with you.

JOHN: Thank you, Miss.

LILIAN: Breeze is a bit sharp.

JOHN: Like yourself, it always is.

LILIAN: That's the worst of the East Coast.

JOHN: I like it. It isn't coy like some places.

LILIAN: Referring to Cheltenham, I suppose.

JOHN: I wasn't thinking of that, no.

LILIAN: Makes a change. Well, what are we going to do?

JOHN: Why did they throw us out?

LILIAN: I suppose they wanted to talk about something. I don't know. To discuss something.

JOHN: They've been married for twenty years. What on earth have they got left to talk about?

LILIAN: Nineteen years.

JOHN: Besides, they could have gone into another part of the house. Or the barn, if they wanted to get away from us. Anyway, they've just had all term.

LILIAN: Probably afraid you'd wander about and poke your nose in as usual.

JOHN: I don't poke my nose in. Hey, you don't suppose they're talking about us, do you?

LILIAN: I shouldn't think so. Why, have you been up to something?

JOHN: No.

LILIAN: Honest?

JOHN: Honest. Well, nothing like that. Nothing they'd care about. What about you? Why always assume it has to be me who's in trouble?

LILIAN: Because you're a boy, because you're younger, and because it usually is.

JOHN: That's true. I've been form captain this term. And I got two prizes.

LILIAN: You said three in your letter.

JOHN: Two. The J. G. Bland Memorial for Reading and the
         Swainson Mathematical Studies.
LILIAN: You must be brighter than you seem.
             [JOHN *gives her a false smile.*]
         They named after Old Boys?
JOHN: Mm. I remember Bland. He was killed last year. Just
         got his commission in the Cavalry. He was our senior
         Under Officer my first term.
LILIAN: Our prizes are all named after former mistresses.
         They give one when they retire.
JOHN: Couldn't have them named after former mistresses in a
         boys' school. It'd cause talk.
LILIAN: Ha-ha!
JOHN: Anyway, you haven't said whether you've been up to
         something.
LILIAN: Course I haven't, stupid.
JOHN: That doesn't sound very grown-up talk to me. Is that
         how you address each other at your convent in the
         Cotswolds?
LILIAN: Good heavens, no, Hockaday. We reserve it exclusively
         for cretins.
JOHN: Most kind.
LILIAN: I'm cold.
JOHN: What time did they say we should go back?
LILIAN: I have to be in the village at three, but you're not to
         turn up until five at the earliest.
JOHN: Why not till five?
LILIAN: Because. Don't sit on that.
JOHN: Why not?
LILIAN: Been in the sea for weeks. Probably covered in things.
         And it'll be soaking.
JOHN: Bleached dry.
LILIAN: There could be seaweed or anything.
JOHN: But there isn't.
             [*He sits down.*]
LILIAN: On your head be it.
JOHN: More likely to be on my bottom.
LILIAN: John!

JOHN: That's what I sit on.

LILIAN: You have no consideration. King Henry's must be a school for guttersnipes from the sound of it.

JOHN: I say, Lily, that's a bit strong.

LILIAN: Well.

JOHN: It is a bit blowy, isn't it? Do you think it's too cold to swim?

LILIAN: You haven't got your things.

JOHN: I could always go and get them.

LILIAN: You're not to go back to the house.

[*Pause. Sound of seabirds.*]

You had a good term, then?

JOHN: Not bad. Yours?

LILIAN: All right. What you doing?

[JOHN *is bringing a piece of wood across the breakwater.*]

JOHN: Making a shelter. You've only got one more year, haven't you?

LILIAN: Yes.

JOHN: You going for Oxford, then?

LILIAN: Don't be silly.

JOHN: Why not?

LILIAN: Wouldn't stand a chance.

JOHN: Course you would, you're a Hockaday.

LILIAN: I'm a female.

JOHN: Doesn't show. Ow! That hurt.

LILIAN: There are hardly any colleges for females.

JOHN: Couldn't Daddy help?

LILIAN: I shouldn't think so. Do you know, he only got a Third? I looked it up.

JOHN: Really? I think he should be more modest in his opinions, then. Fancy being treated by a doctor who only got a Third.

LILIAN: Better than being treated by one who got a Fourth.

JOHN: Or a foreigner.

LILIAN: Mind, it's only the people in the village, and they don't catch much.

JOHN: And the recruits over at Castle Whatnot.

LILIAN: They're not there long. What are you doing with that bit?

JOHN: I'm not sure. Will it stay there? No. So what are you going to do?

LILIAN: I hope they'll let me do a Pitman's course. Then I can become a stenographer or something. I don't want to sit around and become an old maid.

JOHN: Perhaps someone will marry you. Then you won't have to worry.

[LILIAN *does not reply.*]

You could become an old widow, then.

LILIAN: [*quietly*] No.

JOHN: What's that?

LILIAN: Gannet.

JOHN: No, the ship. Look at it.

LILIAN: I don't know. One of ours, I'm sure.

JOHN: Really low in the water.

LILIAN: Probably full of coal or something.

JOHN: That wasn't a gannet. I expect it was a Brent goose or a . . .

LILIAN: Rubbish, it was a gannet. You don't get Brent geese at this time of year. And mind what you're doing.

JOHN: I'm only doing it for you. Have you seen that bi-plane yet? The one that came down.

LILIAN: I only came home the day before you.

JOHN: Why don't we go and do that, then? Be a grand thing to see.

LILIAN: No.

JOHN: Why not?

LILIAN: You haven't finished your shelter.

JOHN: That doesn't matter.

LILIAN: It's the wrong way, it's over towards Ashby, take ages.

JOHN: We've got all afternoon.

LILIAN: I've got to be in the village at three.

JOHN: Do your shopping after.

LILIAN: No.

JOHN: Why not?

LILIAN: No!

JOHN: It's nothing to be frightened of. Only bits of wood and canvas and wires and things all mashed up. They'll have taken the body away.

LILIAN: Don't be horrible.

JOHN: It's true.

LILIAN: I know, but you don't have to say so.
[JOHN *looks at her.*]

JOHN: You shouldn't be afraid of the truth. That's where everyone gets in a mess.

LILIAN: Some things are private.

JOHN: What's that got to do with it?

LILIAN: I'm just saying. You don't have to *say* everything.

JOHN: Course you don't. But you ought to be able to look at it. Straight on. Otherwise you don't know what anything is.

LILIAN: I don't think so. Not if it's going to make you unhappy and cause scars on you too. Some people are sensitive. And for your information, it's nothing to do with bloodstains or soggy limbs that I don't want to go over to Ashby.

JOHN: Don't tell me it's the compelling attraction of the post office and the village store.
[LILIAN *shakes her head.*]
What then?

LILIAN: You don't always have to say.

JOHN: You do to me. I'm your brother.

LILIAN: All right. You tell me why it's so important to go and see this machine.

JOHN: Because it's the greatest thing Man has ever invented.

LILIAN: A broken bi-plane?

JOHN: Oh, things always go wrong if you're going to do anything worthwhile. You must know that. But this has moved us into a whole new element. We did Icarus about a year ago. And you see it was wrong. Wrong, wrong, wrong.

LILIAN: I'm not trying to be clever, but the man in that bi-plane fetched up very much the same as Icarus.

JOHN: Because he made a mistake, or something wasn't strong enough. That doesn't mean there's a fault in the idea. He didn't fall out of the sky because he'd affronted Zeus, a punishment for his ambition; he fell out of the sky because of an error, something that can be corrected. His or somebody else's.

LILIAN: It might have been a judgment of God. We don't know.

JOHN: I do. There isn't a God.

LILIAN: [*quietly*] John.

JOHN: There isn't.

LILIAN: What do you think the Churches are here for? — St. John's and All Saints, and you've got a chapel at school. You can hardly avoid taking notice of them.

JOHN: Who's saying they're not there? I'm not. There are such things as Greek temples and witch doctors. That doesn't prove the beliefs they stand for are true.

LILIAN: Maybe people's needing it is the proof.

JOHN: Or, or, that people haven't been given the choice.

LILIAN: I know, you went to see a Bernard Shaw play this term, didn't you? That's where you got all this from.

JOHN: No I haven't. Didn't like the play, anyway. It was just people sitting around talking. I mean, what kind of play's that? No, I've been thinking.

[LILIAN *looks at him.*]

All the good ideas, the people who had good ideas weren't doing what they were told. They were against what everyone else said they should think. Or do. Because they could see more, more than other people.

LILIAN: Maybe they could. But in the first place they learned everything they could that everyone else had found out and then they worked harder, using their knowledge and their intelligence.

JOHN: No, they experimented, they found out for themselves.

LILIAN: That's not the same as denying what everybody already knows and what's perfectly obvious. How can you experiment if you don't know anything to start with?

JOHN: If you're repeating what's already been proved it's not an experiment.

LILIAN: What is it then, Clever Dick?

JOHN: A test.

LILIAN: So you're testing that God doesn't exist, are you?

JOHN: I don't know.

LILIAN: Well, Descartes has proved that he does to my satisfaction and to that of a great number of other people.

JOHN: I haven't read Descartes.

LILIAN: Well, there you are then.

JOHN: Have you read what the Druids used to do, or what their commandments were?

LILIAN: Of course not. They were pagans.

JOHN: I don't think there's anything in existence they wrote down.

LILIAN: That was a silly question then, wasn't it? I can't read what doesn't exist, so it's no fault of mine.

JOHN: What they believed may have been true, though. Whether it was or not isn't changed by being written down.

LILIAN: Are you going to build this shelter, or are we just going to look at two pieces of driftwood?

JOHN: All I'm saying is truth and what people write down or what they know they know aren't the same thing.

LILIAN: You may have been form captain this term, but I shouldn't be surprised if you end up on the gallows.

[*Short pause.*]

JOHN: Up in the air.

[*He goes and stands on the breakwater, looking out to sea.*]

Air's just like water, really. Only without being wet.

LILIAN: There was a girl at school like you. They put her away. Kindest thing they could do for her.

JOHN: There's a big bit over there.

[*He goes to fetch the driftwood.*]

LILIAN: What happened to Landon-Wood?

JOHN: He's my best friend.

LILIAN: Wasn't he form captain?

JOHN: Yes, last year. He wasn't as good at it as me. But we still chuck together and we're in the same shoot. He's a fearfully good runner, won the Colts' cross-country. His Latin stinks, though. I've given up cribbing from him altogether.

LILIAN: A boy your age shouldn't be cribbing.

JOHN: It's only Latin.

LILIAN: Even so.

JOHN: Goody Two-Shoes.

LILIAN: Some people take the view that there should be a connection between truthfulness and what gets written down, that's all.

JOHN: I didn't say that.

LILIAN: Don't you agree with it, then?

JOHN: Yes.

LILIAN: That's not going to stay there.

[JOHN *adjusts a piece of wood. It falls.*]

Told you.

JOHN: People like Columbus and Galileo, and Turner too, they went against what everybody expected and thought was right.

LILIAN: Yes, but lots of people have done that and been wrong. They were right because they were right, not because they opposed everyone else. And, as it happens, Turner was an R.A.

JOHN: So?

LILIAN: He was an official top dog.

JOHN: Well, Whistler then.

LILIAN: So's he.

JOHN: Not to begin with. They wouldn't have been right if they'd agreed with everything they'd been told when they started, and the world would never have become modern like it has.

LILIAN: John, what kind of trouble are you in?

JOHN: I'm not.

LILIAN: Then why bring this up?

JOHN: Because it matters. And it's interesting. I can't see any more wood.

LILIAN: There's a spar over there.

JOHN: Do you think somebody's been along collecting it?

LILIAN: There may have been an extra high tide swept it all away. Lowestoft harbour is probably blocked with flotsam now. And it'll come back on Saturday week. Back and forth. Back and forth.

JOHN: Probably old Jock.

LILIAN: Until suddenly a fresh current will bear it off to somewhere else. A new ocean or a new shore.

JOHN: Used it for a fire in that hut-place where he stays, near the Butter Cross. Have you seen him this time?

LILIAN: Who?

JOHN: Old Jock.

LILIAN: Not since the Easter holiday when he had that bad chest. I may see him today of course, as it's in the High Street I'm meeting . . .

> [*She trails off suddenly.*]

JOHN: Meeting?

LILIAN: Mm?

JOHN: Who are you meeting?

LILIAN: I was saying I may meet Old Jock.

JOHN: No you weren't.

LILIAN: If he's still about. He's very old now. He's over fifty. And he's never eaten properly.

JOHN: That's why you're going into the village. You brazen hussy!

LILIAN: I'm not!

JOHN: You've got an assignation. I say, you didn't persuade the parents to order us out, did you? Just to ease your arrangements.

LILIAN: Don't tell anyone, John.

JOHN: Course I won't. Who could I tell?

LILIAN: Father.

JOHN: That's insulting.

LILIAN: Thank you, John.

JOHN: There is a code of conduct.

LILIAN: Some of the girls at school can't wait to spread that sort of story about people.

JOHN: Yes, well; that's a girls' school for you. Have you known him long?

LILIAN: I met him on the train from London.

JOHN: What, two days ago, on the way home? That's pretty fast.

LILIAN: It stopped at every station. Oh, sorry.

JOHN: Don't worry. Your secret is safe with me. You didn't notice what time high tide is, did you? I can't work out whether it's meant to be coming in or going out.

LILIAN: Don't you want to know about him?

JOHN: Who?

LILIAN: My young man.

JOHN: Not much, no.

LILIAN: He's with the East Suffolks.

JOHN: Officer?

LILIAN: At present he's in training. He's only been there a few weeks, I'm not sure how many. He's frightfully nice. Very pale and neat, and he speaks quietly.

JOHN: What school was he at?

LILIAN: He was in an orphanage.

JOHN: Good Lord. Does he know how to use a knife and fork and that sort of thing?

LILIAN: Somewhere near Bishop's Stortford. Then he obtained a job as a clerk. Now of course he's volunteered. But he hasn't any family.

JOHN: Some people have all the luck.

LILIAN: He's nowhere to go on leave, so he just has to stay on the camp. We're going to take tea. And he said he'd bring some of his sketches for me to see. He's done lots of drawings, sea views and the countryside, and some of the villages, too, apparently. It was something he started doing when he was thirteen and had to leave the orphanage. He said, sometimes, when he had no money people would let him pay with them. For a meal, or towards the rent of his room. He's very resourceful.

JOHN: It is going out.

LILIAN: He said he'd like to draw me.

JOHN: The waves aren't coming up as far as that weed. They were before.

LILIAN: And he's insisted he'll pay for the tea. He's tremendously nice.

JOHN: You'll have to take care Ma Frost doesn't blab.

LILIAN: Why?

JOHN: You'll be going to the Old Oak Tearooms, won't you? And you know how she likes to tell everyone's business. I expect she went to your school.

LILIAN: I'm not doing anything wrong.

JOHN: No, but if she told Mother and Father.

LILIAN: They'd like him, if only they could understand.

JOHN: That's hopeless.

LILIAN: He's quite handsome. Not very big. But quite handsome.
          Little 'tache.
          [*She runs a finger along part of her top lip. The sound of waves
          breaking.*]
          Your shelter hasn't got very far.

JOHN: Run out of things to build it with.

LILIAN: It's not fair that Ma and Pa wouldn't approve. It's so
          difficult. After all, they got married.

JOHN: They'd known each other for hundreds of years.
          Besides, I don't suppose either of them *approved* even
          then.

LILIAN: They must have. They were in love.

JOHN: I think they probably had nothing better to do. Pater
          needed someone to run the house, supervise the meals
          and so on and Ma . . . well, there wasn't much else she
          could have done. Not in those days. Lucky break for her,
          really.

LILIAN: You'll see.

JOHN: Not me. I'd rather join the Fleet.

LILIAN: Is that what you want to do? The parents wouldn't
          mind that.

JOHN: What I'd actually like to do is learn to be a flier.

LILIAN: That's not a profession.

JOHN: It might be.

LILIAN: Going over enemy lines and dropping bombs on people.
          There won't be anyone left by the time you're old
          enough to do it. The war will be well won.

JOHN: I expect they'll be used for other things.

LILIAN: Like what?

JOHN: I don't know. Taking messages from one place to
          another. And planning how a city is going to be laid out.
          To a fellow up in the air it must look like a map, only the
          buildings are standing up, like that book Grandpapa
          gave us, when you open the pages.

LILIAN: You wouldn't be still long enough. That would be quite
          impractical. Once the fighting's over there won't be any
          more aeroplanes, I'm sure.

JOHN: I expect somebody said that about the wheel, back in Ancient Egypt.

LILIAN: There's no call to be facetious.

JOHN: You sound exactly like Mother.

LILIAN: That's not fair.

JOHN: Well, why do you always have to be against things? 'That won't work.' 'You can't do that.'

LILIAN: I'm not.

JOHN: Yes you are.

LILIAN: You're the one who's against religion. I'm the one who's for it.

JOHN: That's just doing what you're told. If there's anything new, anything that means breaking the rules, you go all proper with a churn of cold butter in your mouth.

LILIAN: Oh yes? You're meeting someone in the village, are you?

JOHN: What do you mean?

LILIAN: I never heard of you having a secret meeting with some young lady.

JOHN: Don't be daft.

LILIAN: I don't think that's stick-in-the-mud of me.

JOHN: That's just lust.

LILIAN: Oh, we believe in the commandments, do we? And it isn't. It's a sincere friendship.

JOHN: So. I've met lots of friends at different times.

LILIAN: That's not the same and you know it. They're all friends you're allowed to mention. And if you're so rebellious, how come you were such a marvellous form captain and won those prizes? That sounds stick-in-the-mud, 'yes sir, no sir' to me.

JOHN: That was excellence. And stop changing the subject.

LILIAN: I'm not changing the subject. I'm simply pointing out that if you want to be Leader of the Opposition you can't be Prime Minister as well.

JOHN: What I want to be, if we can just get back to what we were originally discussing, is the captain of a flying machine. And I probably will be, although *you* say there won't be any.

LILIAN: The aeroplane is the latest grandchild of the crossbow.

JOHN: What?

LILIAN: It was invented to hurtle through the air starting from ground level, just like the bow and arrow, and at some point in the distance to bring about the death of some creature it was aimed at. Unlike the bow, the aeroplane also makes the journey to deliver its arrow, and returns. But the idea's just the same, so's the result, only worse. You even talk of a target in both cases. And in all of history the crossbow has never been put to any other purpose. Nor will the aeroplane.

JOHN: Could have taken Jesus up into heaven. Haven't you ever thought Jesus and Icarus could be the same name. Yaisus. Yakarus.

LILIAN: I'm not sure that isn't blasphemous.

JOHN: Can't be if you're not a believer. Blasphemy is denying the true god. If you know that no god exists that can't be blasphemy. It's thinking different.

LILIAN: That's still blasphemy to other people. You're speaking irreverently of *our* God.

JOHN: That's what de la Hague said.

LILIAN: Your headmaster? You didn't say that to him?

JOHN: A bit more than that.

LILIAN: Oh John, you're the bold challenger.

JOHN: That's why they took away the Divinity Prize.

LILIAN: I was right.

JOHN: You were right.

LILIAN: You had won three.

JOHN: And one from three is two.

LILIAN: Are you awfully upset?
           [JOHN *shakes his head.*]

JOHN: They reward lies, if it makes everyone comfortable. I don't want that. I want the truth.

LILIAN: That's uncompromising, John, very honourable.

JOHN: I can't see the point if you don't want that.

LILIAN: Teachers and people who run things want everyone to believe the same. It makes life simpler, easier to accomplish things I suppose, more efficacious. Also their views may in fact be right. You see, I rather think they are. And everybody punishes people who go wrong.

They always have. I mean, that's reasonable, isn't it?

JOHN: Depends where you're standing. That's why I want to fly. Get a better view. Look, if you were a French revolutionary you should have been doing what the King told you, not storming the Bastille. To take up arms against the King must have been treason, which is really bad. But the rebels won, so it was the King who became the traitor and whose head was cut off. And it was the rebels who made the new laws. So the truth can change sides. Only it can't really. Not the true truth. Not if you worked it out for yourself.

LILIAN: When he was young, Grandfather could have known someone who was alive at the time of the French revolution.

[JOHN *looks at her questioningly.*]

He was born in 1848. Isn't time funny? The storming of the Bastille seems like ancient history. We can almost touch it through Grandfather.

JOHN: Grandfather Hockaday or Grandfather Trent?

LILIAN: Well, either, really. I was thinking of Grandfather Trent. But there's only a year's difference in their ages.

JOHN: Or if you marry your soldier —

LILIAN: Heavens!

JOHN: — Mother and Father would know that was very wrong, but you would tell your children you were absolutely right. Who ought they to believe?

LILIAN: I'm not going to marry him.

JOHN: You know what I mean.

LILIAN: We're only walking out. And don't forget to keep quiet about it. I know you. When you get carried away, you blurt things out.

JOHN: I won't, Lily, I promise I won't.

LILIAN: Well, don't.

[*Short pause.*]

I knew. I can always tell when something's the matter with you. It's the same with Dorothea at school.

[*Pause.*]

They didn't take the prize away because you said the truth was indivisible. That's part of the teaching.

JOHN: To win it you had to do three things: learn a psalm and recite it without a mistake, ours was 15, it varied with what year you're in; sight-read a passage they suddenly put in front of you; and do a test on the parables. There was only one prize for the whole school. So I did all that and I won it and they gave it to me. Then they took it away.

LILIAN: Why?

    [Sound of a hooter out to sea.]

JOHN: What's that?

LILIAN: Probably the coaster that goes round to Lynn each week. Yes, look.

    [Sound of waves.]

JOHN: We had to write an essay for prep. on the Crusades. And I said how funny it was that both sides were dying for God and trying to stamp out pagans. And nobody was doing anything stupid like turning the other cheek. Not if they could help it. They were too busy killing for Jesus. Then it dawned on me. Forgiveness and all that stuff's just a fiction. Religion's something you kill for: Saracens, Mohammedans; Jews because they crucified Jesus; Catholics because we're Protestants; Protestants because we're Catholics; Catholics because we're the Inquisition and they're not such good Catholics; Protestants because we're Protestants too, but we've got a different King, and bigger ships. Everybody's been doing it since the world began. Abraham would have killed his son to be let off detention. In the name of goodness. And truth. And God. That's not goodness and truth. That's wickedness. I know. That's a lie.

LILIAN: But all the really good people have been religious. You mustn't forget that.

JOHN: That's the biggest lie. Some of them were forced. And I expect there's lots we haven't been told about. Lots of people like Socrates. He was there long before Jesus or the Mahdi. And he didn't claim to be anything special. He said, question things. So I thought, if we're all God's children why is it right for one half of us to kill the other half all the time? And I thought of Bland. He was good at rugby, superb at running. His legs don't move now.

Jesus must be pleased. He's just a photograph stuck in the front of a book with a scroll round it. And everybody says it's all right because he's gone to heaven. Well, why didn't he go straight there in the first place? Why did he bother to go to King Henry's and play rugger first? And where do the good Huns go? Do they go to heaven too? And when they meet Bland and Kitchener and people, do they go on fighting, and if it isn't all right to go on fighting in heaven how is it all right to go on fighting on earth? When you look at someone who's dead, they don't look as though they're in heaven. Especially after six days — remember that lobster fisherman who capsized last year? He just looked rotted, and bloated, and empty.

LILIAN: That was being in the water all that time.

JOHN: We're just like flowers or trees or animals or anything else. When we're alive, we're alive, and when we're dead, we're nothing. Nobody *knows* any more than that, for all that they pretend. And I think if people realized that, they'd treat life as more valuable, other people's lives, too. It's a good thing. It shouldn't be thrown away on the chance of a non-existent heaven. Or wasted doing endless parsing and figures of speech.

LILIAN: But then there'd be no Last Judgment. Everyone could be immoral with no consequences.

JOHN: No. People use heaven like a safety net and it makes them careless — they don't care. If they thought that life is all there is, it's like a tightrope, they wouldn't be so keen to push people off in case they got pushed off back. They'd value life and they'd mind what they did with it. They'd know how special it is; and the consequences are here.

LILIAN: That's not enough. What would anyone believe in?

JOHN: Now. And tomorrow.

LILIAN: Our Mother Superior would go mad if she heard that. Mind you, she's somewhere on the way, anyway.

JOHN: King Henry's wasn't thrilled. De la Hague saw my essay and said I couldn't have the Divinity Prize after that.

LILIAN: You must admit it's a very heretical view.

JOHN: King Henry's is a C of E School. We're all heretics there.

LILIAN: Heathen, then.

JOHN: I've got to understand what I believe. It's got to make sense.

LILIAN: Do the parents know? Have you told them?

JOHN: [*shaking his head*] I think it's too complicated for them.

LILIAN: You will end up on the gallows.

JOHN: That's the last thing I intend to do. Is your soldier very patient?

LILIAN: Why?

JOHN: If you were meeting him at three, he's only been waiting a couple of minutes so far, according to the clock tower.

LILIAN: Oh Lord!

[*She starts gathering her things and then straightening herself.*]

JOHN: Mind he doesn't give you a baby.

LILIAN: John!

JOHN: Well, you're obviously sweet on him and I expect you're going to spoon and things.

LILIAN: Mind your own business.

JOHN: I am. I'm not ready to be an uncle.

LILIAN: Just think what you're going to do this afternoon. Don't worry about me.

JOHN: But, Lilian, I do worry. I'll be looking at the bi-plane and I don't want anything to go wrong with your hanky-panky. I mean, if he starts kissing you, be careful. If he kisses you in a special way, you could get a baby.

LILIAN: John.

[*She looks at him pityingly.*]

I know that.

[*She goes.* JOHN *watches her. Then he throws a pebble or two towards the sea. He lies back. The light fades. The sound of waves breaking.*]

THE END